THE EASY SECTION 609 CREDIT REPAIR SECRET

REMOVE ALL NEGATIVE ACCOUNTS IN 30 DAYS USING A FEDERAL LAW LOOPHOLE THAT WORKS EVERY TIME

By

BRANDON WEAVER

www.609creditrepair.com

D1711001

INTRODUCTION

I have had my own problems with credit and I wish I had known about the Section 609 of the Fair Credit Reporting Act. It would have saved me a lot of stress and worry. It would have saved me YEARS of my life. I'm hoping this has found you sooner rather than later, but I suppose it doesn't truly matter because now you have it. And it's going to work!

Healing your credit is not hard. It's pretty easy and you don't need anyone else to help you do it. This book is going to teach you how to do it yourself. It's going to give you your power back and give you back your life.

Many times, without a good credit score you can't get a nice apartment, you can't get utilities turned on, you can't get a phone, you can't get cable or internet, you can't get a good rate on a car loan or house loan, you can't get a good credit card that gives you rewards back on purchases, so it's a very important financial tool that can work for you or hurt you. I want your FICO score to help you from now on.

This eBook with the letters that will help you clean up your credit. They are simple and straight forward, but they WILL work. Your individual results will vary, and it may take a few rounds of letter writing, but this style of dispute will heal your credit. Continue to use this method for all the adverse accounts on your credit reports until your credit is completely clean and your FICO score is where you need it to be.

TABLE OF CONTENTS

Introduction

Table of Contents

Legal Notes

Why it Works

What to Expect

Getting Started Cleaning Up Your Credit

Dispute Letters

Level 1 Dispute Letter Template

Level 2 Dispute Letter Template

Level 3 Dispute Letter Template

Level 4 Dispute Letter Template

Conclusion

Thanks

About The Author

Other Books By Brandon

WHY IT WORKS

Equifax, Experian, and TransUnion are the 3 main Credit Reporting Agencies or CRA's. Learn their names – well if you don't know their names by now you will. Anyway, when you use a credit card or get a loan or do any type of credit transaction with a bank or credit card company this information is typically sent to the CRA's. This information is placed into your credit report using your Social Security Number.

You should understand that this type of reporting is all electronic. There is no paperwork, it's all digital. There is never a verification of any signed documents or contracts or anything. Every month, without fail, banks and credit card companies send electronic files with details of your account to the CRA's. The Credit Reporting Agencies or bureaus place this information into your credit report without VERIFICATION. No one is checking if this account is really yours. No one is checking if the information is CORRECT. No one is checking on the banks or creditors to make sure that they are doing the right thing.

Interesting...

Equifax, Experian and TransUnion believe the banks and credit card companies are reporting properly. This could be true, but without verification no one is sure. The U.S. Government realized this was a problem and so came about THE FAIR CREDIT REPORTING ACT (FCRA). The FCRA is the law for CRA's. This law is going to protect your rights as a citizen of the United States of America.

The FCRA states the bureaus must verify all information that they get from banks, credit card companies, etc before it's put into your credit report. What the CRA's must have is the ORGINAL SIGNED DOCUMENT from when you opened your credit card or got your loan. But since all that paperwork for millions of accounts would be impossible to verify, not to mention how expensive it would be to do so, no one is verifying accounts in this manner. No verification of original signed contract document ever happens between CRA's and creditors.

If you ask to VERIFY, the information the bureaus will end an electronic communication to the creditor asking if the information is correct and the creditor will most likely say "Yes." But no one is looking at ORGINAL SIGNED CONTRACTS.

No one knows this takes places (except for those in the know and you are now in the know). The CRA's are in violation of the FCRA but since people don't know their rights the Credit Reporting Agencies don't do anything about this.

But now armed with this new information YOU will be able to help yourself.

Many of the adverse items on a credit report may in fact be true. So, if you were to dispute the adverse items with a traditional dispute process most of those accounts will be "verified" and will stay on your credit report thus in turn keeping your FICO score down.

That is NOT what you are going to do. And never dispute your credit reports online.

SECTION 609 of the Fair Credit Reporting Act does not care whether the negative account is valid or not. The letter disputes the CRA's right to REPORT the adverse account – NOT whether the adverse account is valid.

These letters will request, under SECTION 609 of the Fair Credit Reporting Act, that the CRA's send you a copy of the original contract that you signed – that they are supposed to have. I mean, if they are verifying the account as being valid/correct then they, by law, are supposed to have a copy of that contract to do so. BUT THEY DON'T.

And since they don't they can't provide you a copy nor can they legally verify the account. Under the Fair Credit Reporting Act they must provide you a copy if you request it. Since they will not be able to provide you such a document the account will be UNVERIFIED and under Federal Law any UNVERIFIED accounts must be deleted.

Remember, your results will vary depending how many accounts you need to dispute and so forth and so on. You may send 1 rounds of letters and get everything removed or it may take 4 rounds of letters to get everything removed. It is important to keep going. And to keep sending the letters. Be prepared to go a few rounds of letter sending.

WHAT TO EXPECT

When you send your notarized letters to Experian, TransUnion, and Equifax they might try to ignore you and send you a reply saying a suspicious letter was sent on your behalf but has been ignored or may try to intimidate you to stop you from continuing your disputes. However, you must keep going.

I have personally seen this reply:

"We received a suspicious request regarding your personal credit information that

we have determined was not sent by you. We have not taken any action on this

request and any future requests made in this manner will not be processed and will

not receive a response."

All the letters you send will be notarized and have tracking on them. Sending them priority is a good idea if you want to get things cleared up fast. Priority mail comes with tracking and gets to the CRA's in a few days instead of weeks. All the letters will also have a copy of your Social Security Card and Driver License so how did they determine it was not you who sent the letter?

They didn't. It's just a scare tactic. So, listen to me – KEEP GOING.

You might also get something like this:

"Suspicious requests are taken seriously and reviewed by security personnel who will

report deceptive activity, including copies of letters deemed as suspicious, to law

enforcement officials and to state or federal regulatory agencies."

Just another scare tactic. They may also ask for proof of your identity and request you mail them such proof. But you already sent a notarized letter with your SS Card and ID so what's the problem?

KEEP GOING!

There is no doubt it's you, they are stalling and trying to scare you. Just send your next round of letters and emphasis this is your 2nd (or 3rd or 4th) request and you will seek legal actions. Keep demanding that Equifax, Experian, and TransUnion truly verify your accounts with a signed copy of your original contracts. If they don't do so they must delete the adverse accounts.

In the event they ignore you all together you can file a lawsuit and sue the bureaus. You can file your complaint here:

https://www.ftccomplaintassistant.gov

GETTING STARTED CLEANING UP YOUR CREDIT

The United States Government allows a free credit report from Experian, Equifax, and TransUnion once a year (a 12 month period from when you pull the reports, not a calender year). You can get those reports here: http://www.annualcreditreport.com

Now that you have your credit reports (whether you got them free or had to pay for a report you need it to dispute adverse accounts) identify all the adverse items to remove.

Go to the dispute letters for Experian, Equifax and TransUnion and copy the adverse information from your credit reports into the letters to send to the CRA's. Only dispute 22 adverse accounts at one time. Trying to dispute more than that could make the CRA's classify the dispute as frivolous.

EXAMPLE: You have 10 adverse accounts on your TransUnion report. Go to the TransUnion letter 1, type it up and add the 10 adverse accounts you want removed. Do this for Equifax, and Experian and then you will need to get it them all notarized.

Now you need to get the letter(s) notarized. You will add a copy of your social security card and Driver License (or passport) for proof of your identity and go a notary of the public. DO NOT SIGN THE LETTERS UNTIL YOU GO TO THE NOTARY AND THEY TELL YOU TO SIGN IT. Now your letters are ready to send.

You will send your letter WITH TRACKING your choices are Priority Mail (my personal favorite) or Certified Mail. This is your proof the CRA's get your dispute letter(s).

Now you wait. Wait for the response in the mail and if you don't get all the adverse accounts removed and the bureaus didn't give you any written verification as proof then KEEP GOING. Send the next letter in the system.

I recommend you keep 3 folders. 1 for each Credit Reporting Agency and keep all the receipts with the tracking numbers, copies of the responses, copy of the letters you send, notes, etc. You need a paper trail, because if you need to sue you will need proof. Hopefully, it doesn't come to this but evidence will be invaluable should such a thing need to occur.

DISPUTE LETTERS

The templates for the dispute letters are below. As this is a Kindle book (it keeps the price lower to help more people) you will have to type these letters yourself. However, they will work – I've done it myself.

Below are the addresses you will use for the credit bureaus, Equifax, Experian, and TransUnion.

You will need to send a level 1 letter to all 3 bureaus. Then you will need to send a level 2 letter to all 3 bureaus. Then a level 3 letter to all 3 bureaus. And if you still have not gotten all the adverse accounts off your credit score you will need to send a level 4 letter to all 3 bureaus.

Equifax

P.O. Box 740256

Atlanta, GA 30374

Experian

P.O. Box 2002

Allen, TX 75013

Trans Union

P.O. Box # 2000

Chester, PA. 19022

The Level 1 letter template is below. It is two pages. All your letters will be two pages long.

The Level 2 letter template is next after the Level 1 letter template and so forth and so on.

Level 1 Dispute Letter Template

DATE

Your Name

Address

City, State Zip

SSN: 000-00-0000 | DOB: 1/1/1970

CREDIT REPORTING AGENCY

PO BOX ADDRESS

CITY, STATE ZIP CODE

According to the Fair Credit Reporting Act, **Section 609 (a)(1)(A), you are required by federal law to verify -** through the physical verification of the original signed consumer contract - any and all accounts you post on a credit report. Otherwise, anyone paying for your reporting services could fax, mail or email in a fraudulent account.

I demand to see Verifiable Proof (**an original Consumer Contract with my Signature on it**) you have on file of the accounts listed below. Your failure to positively verify these accounts has hurt my ability to obtain credit. Under the FCRA, unverified accounts must be removed and if you are unable to provide me a copy of verifiable proof, you must remove the accounts listed below.

I demand the following accounts be verified or removed immediately.

Account	Account Number	Provide Physical Verification
Creditor 1	1234567890	Unverified Account
Creditor 2	etc	Unverified Account
Creditor 3		Unverified Account
Creditor 4		Unverified Account
Creditor 5		Unverified Account
Creditor 6		Unverified Account
Creditor 7		Unverified Account
Creditor 8		Unverified Account
Creditor 9		Unverified Account
Creditor 10		Unverified Account

* Please remove all **non-account holding inquiries** over 30 days old.

* Please add a **Promotional Suppression** to my credit file.

Thank You,

{YOUR NAME HERE}

IN WITNESS WHEREOF, the said party has signed and sealed these presents the day and year first above written.

Signed, sealed and delivered in the presence of:

{PRINT YOUR NAME HERE}

_____

Signature

STATE OF
COUNTY OF

I HEREBY CERTIFY that on this day before me, an officer duly qualified to take acknowledgments, personally appeared { YOUR NAME HERE }, who has produced _____ as identification and who executed the foregoing instrument and he/she acknowledged before me that he/she executed the same.

WITNESS my hand and official seal in the County and State aforesaid this _____ day of _____ 2018.

_____

Notary Public

Printed Name

My commission expires:

COPY of SSN CARD

COPY OF ID CARD

LEVEL 2 DISPUTE LETTER TEMPLATE

DATE

Your Name

Address

City, State Zip

SSN: 000-00-0000 | DOB: 1/1/1970

CREDIT REPORTING AGENCY

PO BOX ADDRESS

CITY, STATE ZIP CODE

Please be advised this is my SECOND WRITTEN REQUEST. The unverified items listed below remain on my credit report in violation of Federal Law. You are required under the FCRA to have a copy of the original creditors documentation on file to verify that this information is mine and is correct. In the results of your first investigation, you stated in writing that you **"verified"** that these items are being **"reported correctly"** ? Who verified these accounts?

You have **NOT** provided me a copy of ANY original documentation required under **Section 609 (a)(1)(A)** & **Section 611 (a)(1)(A)** (a consumer contract with my signature on it) and

Section 611 (5)(A) of the FCRA – you are required to *"...promptly DELETE all information which cannot be verified."*

The law is very clear as to the Civil liability and the remedy available to me for "negligent noncompliance" **(Section 617)** if you fail to comply. **I am a litigious consumer and fully intend on pursuing litigation in this matter to enforce my rights under the FCRA**

I demand the following accounts be verified or deleted immediately.

Account	Account Number	Provide Physical Verification
Creditor 1	1234567890	Unverified Account
Creditor 2	etc	Unverified Account
Creditor 3		Unverified Account
Creditor 4		Unverified Account
Creditor 5		Unverified Account
Creditor 6		Unverified Account

* Please remove all **non-account holding inquiries** over 30 days old.

* Please add a **Promotional Suppression** to my credit file.

Thank You,

{YOUR NAME HERE}

   IN WITNESS WHEREOF, the said party has signed and sealed these presents the day and year first above written.

Signed, sealed and delivered in the presence of:

{PRINT YOUR NAME HERE}

_____

Signature

STATE OF
COUNTY OF

    I HEREBY CERTIFY that on this day before me, an officer duly qualified to take acknowledgments, personally appeared { YOUR NAME HERE }, who has produced
_____ as identification and who executed the foregoing instrument and he/she acknowledged before me that he/she executed the same.

    WITNESS my hand and official seal in the County and State aforesaid this _____ day of _____ 2018.

_____

Notary Public

Printed Name

My commission expires:

COPY OF ID CARD

COPY of SSN CARD

LEVEL 3 DISPUTE LETTER TEMPLATE

DATE

Your Name

Address

City, State Zip

SSN: 000-00-0000 | DOB: 1/1/1970

CREDIT REPORTING AGENCY

PO BOX ADDRESS

CITY, STATE ZIP CODE

Please be advised this is my THIRD WRITTEN REQUEST and FINAL WARNING that I fully intend to pursue litigation in accordance with the FCRA to enforce my rights and seek relief and recover all monetary damages that I may be entitled to under Section 616 and Section 617 regarding your continued willful and negligent noncompliance.

Despite two written requests, the unverified items listed below still remain on my credit report in violation of Federal Law. You are required under the FCRA to have a copy of the original creditors documentation on file to verify that this information is mine and is correct. In the results of your first investigation and subsequent reinvestigation, you stated in writing that you **"verified"** that these items are being **"reported correctly"** ? Who verified these accounts? You have **NOT** provided me a copy of ANY original documentation (a consumer contract with my signature on it) as required under **Section 609 (a)(1)(A) & Section 611 (a)(1)(A).** Furthermore you have failed to provide the method of verification as required under **Section 611 (a)**

(7). Please be advised that under **Section 611 (5)(A)** of the FCRA – you are required to *"...promptly DELETE all information which cannot be verified."*

The law is very clear as to the Civil liability and the remedy available to me **(Section 616 & 617)** if you fail to comply with Federal Law. I am a litigious consumer and fully intend on pursuing litigation in this matter to enforce my rights under the FCRA.

I demand the following accounts be verified or deleted immediately.

Account	Account Number	Provide Physical Verification
Creditor 1	1234567890	Unverified Account
Creditor 2	etc	Unverified Account
Creditor 3		Unverified Account
Creditor 4		Unverified Account

* Please remove all **non-account holding inquiries** over 30 days old.

* Please add a **Promotional Suppression** to my credit file.

Thank You,

{YOUR NAME HERE}

   IN WITNESS WHEREOF, the said party has signed and sealed these presents the day and year first above written.

Signed, sealed and delivered in the presence of:

{PRINT YOUR NAME HERE}

_____

Signature

STATE OF
COUNTY OF

     I HEREBY CERTIFY that on this day before me, an officer duly qualified to take acknowledgments, personally appeared { YOUR NAME HERE }, who has produced _____ as identification and who executed the foregoing instrument and he/she acknowledged before me that he/she executed the same.

     WITNESS my hand and official seal in the County and State aforesaid this _____ day of _____ 2018.

_____

Notary Public

Printed Name

My commission expires:

COPY OF ID CARD

COPY of SSN CARD

LEVEL 4 DISPUTE LETTER TEMPLATE

DATE

Your Name

Address

City, State Zip

SSN: 000-00-0000 | DOB: 1/1/1970

CREDIT REPORTING AGENCY

PO BOX ADDRESS

CITY, STATE ZIP CODE

NOTICE OF PENDING LITIGATION SEEKING RELIEF AND MONETARY DAMAGES UNDER FCRA SECTION 616 & SECTION 617

Please accept this final written OFFER OF SETTLEMENT BEFORE LITIGATION as my attempt to amicably resolve your continued violation of the Fair Credit Reporting Act regarding your refusal to delete UNVERIFIED information from my consumer file. I intend to pursue litigation in accordance with the FCRA to seek relief and recover all monetary damages that I may be entitled to under Section 616 and Section 617 if the UNVERIFIED items listed below are not deleted immediately. A copy of this letter as well as copies of the three written letters sent to you previously will also become part of a formal complaint to the Federal Trade Commission and shall be used as evidence in pending litigation provided you fail to comply with this offer of settlement.

Despite three written requests, the unverified items listed below still remain on my credit report in violation of Federal Law. You are required under the FCRA to have a copy of the original creditors documentation on file to verify that this information is mine and is correct. In the results of your investigations, you stated in writing that you **"verified"** that these items are being **"reported correctly"?** Who verified these accounts? You have **NOT** provided me a copy of ANY original documentation (a consumer contract with my signature on it) as required under **Section 609 (a)(1)(A) & Section 611 (a)(1)(A).** Furthermore you have failed to provide the method of verification as required under **Section 611 (a) (7).** Please be advised that under **Section 611 (5)(A)** of the FCRA – you are required to *"...promptly DELETE all information which cannot be verified."*

The law is very clear as to the Civil liability and the remedy available to me **(Section 616 & 617)** if you fail to comply with Federal Law. I am a litigious consumer and fully intend on pursuing litigation in this matter to enforce my rights under the FCRA.

I demand the following accounts be verified or deleted immediately.

Account	Account Number	Provide Physical Verification
Creditor 1	1234567890	Unverified Account
Creditor 2	etc	Unverified Account
Creditor 3		Unverified Account

Creditor 4		Unverified Account

* Please remove all **non-account holding inquiries** over 30 days old.

* Please add a **Promotional Suppression** to my credit file.

Thank You,

{YOUR NAME HERE}

IN WITNESS WHEREOF, the said party has signed and sealed these presents the day and year first above written.

Signed, sealed and delivered in the presence of:

{PRINT YOUR NAME HERE}

_____

Signature

STATE OF

COUNTY OF

I HEREBY CERTIFY that on this day before me, an officer duly qualified to take acknowledgments, personally appeared { YOUR NAME HERE }, who has produced

_____ as identification and who executed the foregoing instrument and he/she acknowledged before me that he/she executed the same.

WITNESS my hand and official seal in the County and State aforesaid this _____ day of _____ 2018.

_____

Notary Public

Printed Name

My commission expires:

COPY of SSN CARD

COPY OF ID CARD

CONCLUSION

This process will work. You will have to stay on top of all the dispute letters, but this will improve your FICO score so please, please, please, stay on it. I know it's not the easiest to type up all your letters, but it will be totally worth it!

Thank you so very much for trusting me with your credit health!

Wishing you the best,

Brandon

THANKS

Thank you to all the people who helped me get my credit score back on track. Thank you to all the people who helped me get my financial life on track. Thank you to my girlfriend, my parents, my friends and family you all have helped me so much over the years! Thanks to the Universe!!!

AND THAT YOU TO YOU READER FOR BUYING THIS BOOK!

ABOUT THE AUTHOR

Brandon Weaver is a former soldier who enlisted in the U.S. Army Reserve at the age of 17. He is an accomplished actor having appeared on *Sean Saves The World, We Are Men, iCarly, Victorious, Sam & Cat,* and *Game Shakers.* Along with being an author and actor, Brandon is an entrepreneur, speaker, and investor.

OTHER BOOKS BY BRANDON

How to Remove Hard Inquiries from Credit Reports

How to Remove Bankruptcy and Other Public Records

CAN I ASK A FAVOR?

If you liked this book, found it helpful or otherwise useful then I'd really appreciate it if you would post a review on Amazon. I read all the reviews personally so that I improve.

Thanks for your support!

WWW.609CREDITREPAIR.COM

Made in the USA
San Bernardino, CA
06 May 2018